Sight Words for Kindergarten Coloring Book

Coloring pages with kindergarten sight words to help with sight word practice.

Published By
RW Squared Media

© 2016 J.D. Ware

Directions:

Each page will teach one sight word. The sight word will be accompanied with a practice sheet or with an adorable animal helper. Children can color in the helpers and the sight words to help with memorization. Pages can be used like flash cards for review once colored.

they

They They
They
they they
they

went

Went Went
Went
went went
went

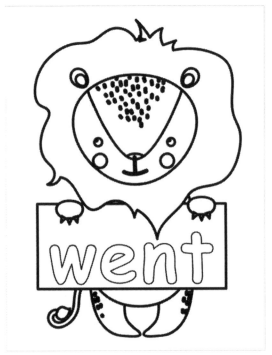

Dolch Kindergarten Sight Words

all	four	out	this
am	get	please	too
are	good	pretty	under
at	have	ran	want
ate	he	ride	was
be	into	saw	well
black	like	say	went
brown	must	she	what
but	new	so	white
came	no	soon	who
did	now	that	will
do	on	there	with
eat	our	they	yes

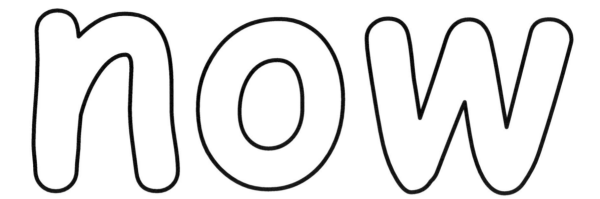

Now Now Now

Now

now now now

now

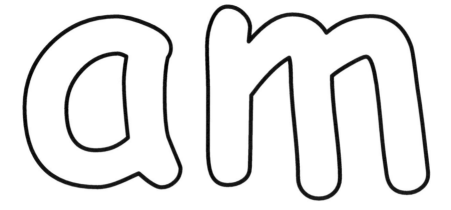

A m A m

A m

a m a m

a m

Too T̤o̤o̤

T̤o̤o̤

too t̤o̤o̤

B e B e

B e

b e b e

b e

On On

On

on on

on

Ate Ate

Ate

ate ate

ate

Into Into

Into Into

into into

into

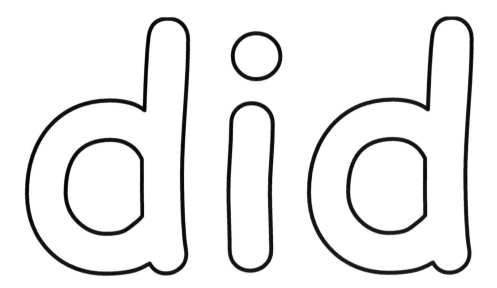

Did Did

Did

did did

did

Get Get

get

black

Black Black

Black

black black

black

brown

Brown Brown

Brown

brown brown

brown

So

So So

So

So So

So

With With

With

with with

with

Want Want

Want

want want

want

there

There There

There

there there

there

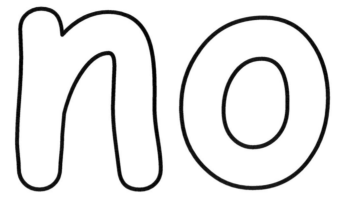

No No

No

no no

no

Who Who

Who

who who

who

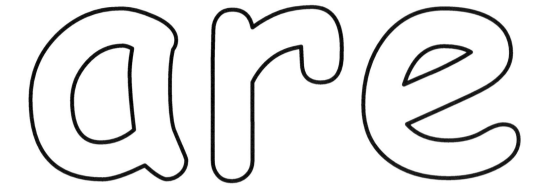

Are Are

Are

are are

are

Went *Went*

Went

went *went*

went

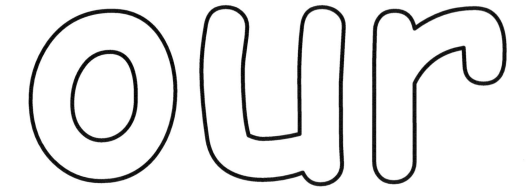

Our Our

Our

our our

our

please

Please Please

Please

please please

please

pretty

Pretty Pretty

Pretty

pretty pretty

pretty

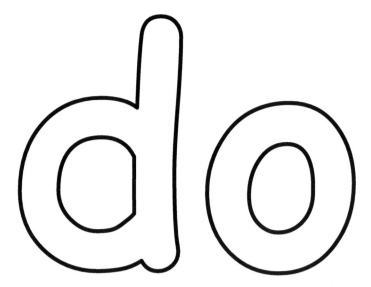

D o D o

D o

d o d o

d o

under

Under Under Under

Under

under under

under

What What

What

what what

what

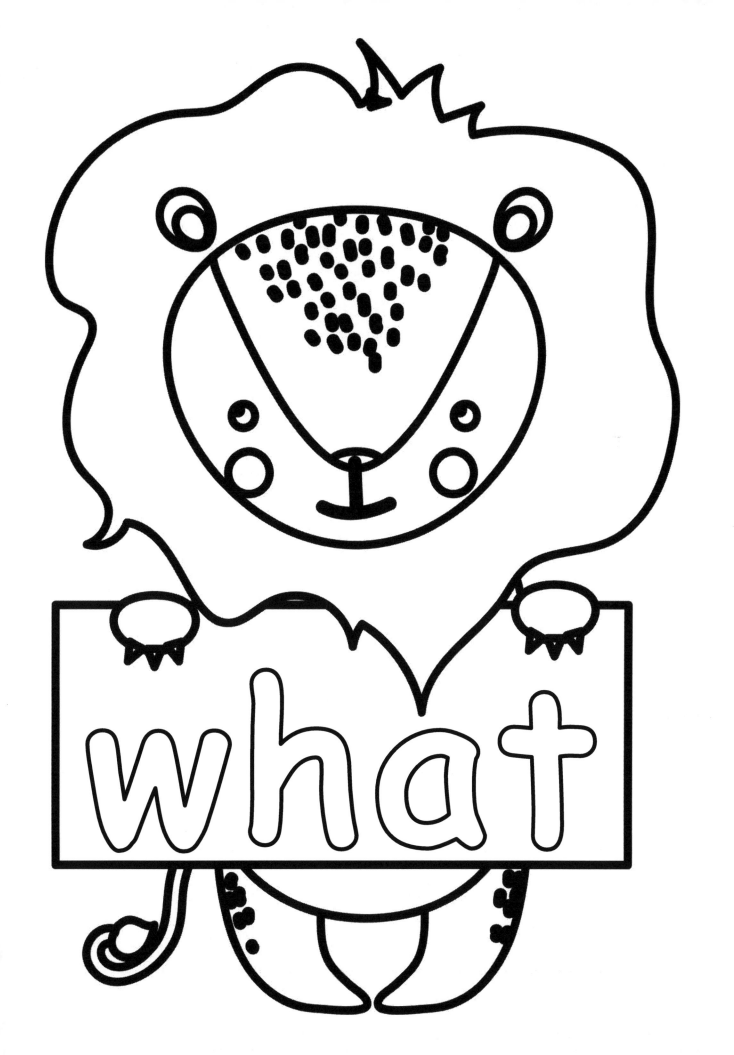

Eat Eat

Eat

eat eat

eat

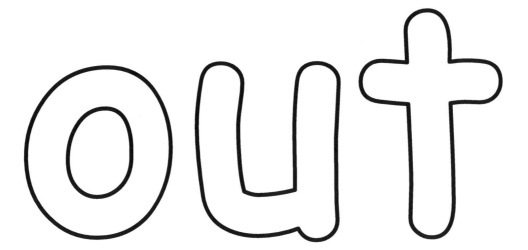

Out Out

Out

out out

out

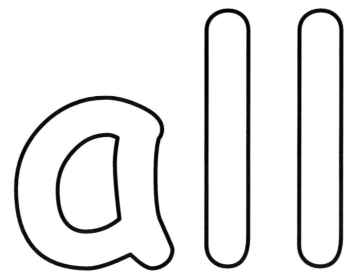

All All

All

all all

all

Must Must

Must

must must

must

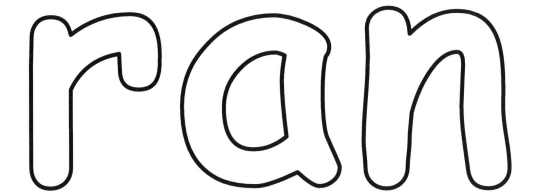

Ran Ran

Ran

ran ran

ran

saw

Saw Saw

Saw

saw saw

saw

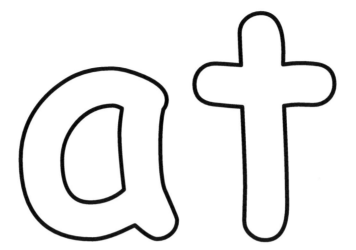

At At At

At

at at

at

Have Have

Have

have have

have

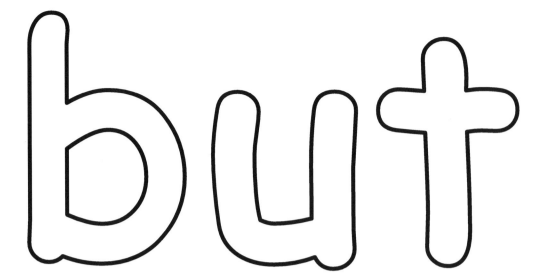

But But

But

but but

but

Say

Say Say

Say

say say

say

White White

White

white white

white

Soon

Soon Soon

Soon

soon soon

soon

She She

She

she she

she

Yes Yes

Yes

yes yes

yes

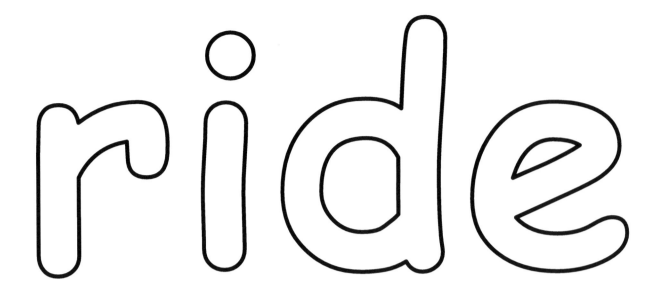

Ride  Ride

Ride

ride  ride

ride

Well Well

Well

well well

well

new

New New

New

new new

new

was

Was Was

Was

was was

was

He   He

He

he   he

he

That That

That

that that

that

This This

This

this this

this

Like ⌐Like⌐

⌐Like

like ⌐like

⌐like

Will Will

Will

will will

will

They They

They

they they

they

came

Came Came

Came

came came

came

Four Four

Four

four four

four

good

Good ~~Good~~

~~Good~~

good ~~good~~

~~good~~

Additional Sight Words Coloring Books
Available online at:
Amazon.com
CreateSpace.com
RWSquaredMedia.WordPress.com

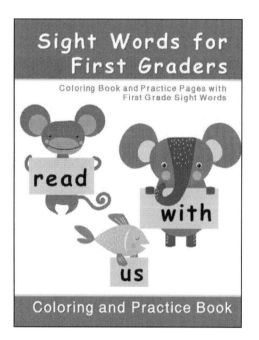

Download free accompanying sight word lists and practice sheets from:

RWSquaredMedia.Wordpress.com/Free-Sight-Words-List

Dedicated to Priscilla. It's been a pleasure watching you learn and grow. You make me so very proud!

Made in the USA
Coppell, TX
28 February 2023

13541174R00063